SPIC

MIXE

book is a

39 SPICES AND HERBS MIXES FROM AROUND THE WORLD THAT EVERY CHEF SHOULD KNOW

SUSANNAH MARIN

TABLE OF CONTENTS

INTRODUCTION

This book will take you on a journey about spices and herbs from around the world, starting from their history, exploration, various uses in the ancient times and about their value since the beginning of the human race, bringing you into the modern world explaining today's trend in the uses and application of spices and herbs.

The chapters in this book will provide you with a wide variety of dry spice mix recipes from around the world, so that you can spice up your meals with any flavor you want, whether it be ethnic, Asian, European, African, etc. You name it and the book has it.

The recipes can be doubled or tripled to fit your need, and in short, provides you with a wide canvas to play with and add your variations. For those who have only entered into the spice world, this book provides various steps explaining how to store the spices, in what form to purchase them, and how to start developing your own blends representing your unique taste.

I hope you enjoy it!

SPICES AND HERBS

A WORLD OF FLAVOR AND AROMATICS

Spices and herbs are a wide source of good flavors. Spices are the aromatic parts of a plant, containing high concentration of flavors, which are primarily used to season, color, and flavor foods. The extraordinary thing about spices is that these are obtained from almost all parts of a plant and might be dried roots, seeds, bark, pod, flowers, fruit, resin or berry. Along with flavoring, spices have a history of being used for medicinal, religious, cosmetics, or for the purpose of making perfumes. Even today, spices are a very important part of many economies. Spices and herbs are often used interchangeably, whereas, unlike spices which can come mostly from all dried parts of a plant, herbs on the other hand, are the leafy green parts of a plant (either dried or fresh), used for food, garnish, medicines, perfume or flavoring.

In the vast use of herbs, the two distinguished uses are medicinal and culinary. For use in medicines, any part of a plant can be considered a herb, whereas, for culinary purpose, herbs from all plants except for the woody plants are used to provide flavor to the food when used in small amount, while providing flavor rather than substance. Some plants are both herbs and spices, and some herbs can be used for both purposes whether it be culinary or medicinal.

HISTORY AND ORIGIN OF SPICES AND HERBS IN THE ANCIENT TIMES

The history of spices and herbs is as old as the history of the human race. The vast uses of spices and herbs have deep roots in the human history along with high value for all cultures. Their use had been handed down from generations to generation from the ancient times. Spices and herbs had been used even before their use had been recorded. Their history is interwoven with adventure, exploring, religious missions, trade and conquest. They have been used by people since the earliest of times, in ancient times, hailed for their medicinal properties.

Spices and herbs were believed to help with problems ranging from a stomach ache to infections and preserving meats, while playing a pivotal role in the development of modern civilization. Ancient civilizations have used spices from time immemorial. The earliest record of their use comes from Egypt, China and India around 6000 years ago.

Many of the world's most coveted spices originated from the tropical areas of the world, mainly the north and south equators. They grew wild and over thousands of years. Their inability to be grown in the harsh weather of Europe made them more exotic and desirable, and much sought after in the west, which incredibly changed the course of history. Because of their scarcity in Europe, they had an enormous trade value. After Europe entered in the spice trade during the 16th century, spices became more widely available there.

Wars have been fought over the spices that we use to flavor our food today, and through the spice trade, spices from one origin of the world have been transferred to the other origins, providing them with their numerous benefits and uplifting their economies. Arab traders travelled through Southeast Asia and brought the valued spices to Greek.

East, including China, Southeast Asia and India is the birthplace of many popular spices and herbs such as: anise, cardamom, basil, garlic, clove, ginger, nutmeg, peppers, and onion.

Whereas, spices like bay leaf, cumin, dill, fenugreek, rosemary, sesame, sage and thyme came from the Middle East, Africa and other parts of the Mediterranean. The colder European regions were the home to juniper and horseradish.

MODERN WORLD TRENDS IN SPICES AND HERBS

Changing immigration patterns, and opening of trade routes have changed the way modern people eat. There is a revolutionary change in eating patterns and the use of spices. People's interest in flavors from faraway has increased. They are interested in exploring the flavors of other countries and cultures. Unlike the old times, the foods and ingredients of south East Asia, china, India, North America and Mediterranean are more common now.

Diversity in the American culture and of the world as a whole, has brought a change in flavor perception of the people. Now, the spices from different regions are easily available to people who want to taste the cuisine of other cultures.

Spices and herbs are increasingly used in pharmaceuticals. New ways are being paved to fight various diseases and illnesses.

Since there are a large number of spices and herbs that are used in cooking around the world, and as there are many common spices and herbs among different cuisines, a number of famous and most commonly used spices that are originated from different parts of the world such as Asian, Mediterranean, African, American, European, etc., are mentioned below.

Asafetida, Bay leaves, Cardamom, Cinnamon, Cloves, Curry leaves, Lime leaves, Kalenjin, Vietnamese, coriander, Lemongrass, Saffron, Sesame leaves, Star anise, Turmeric, Shiso, Papal, Allspice, Hot pepper, Basil, Sage leaves, Parsley, Thyme, Oregano, Paprika, Black, white and cayenne Peppers, Nutmeg, Vanilla, Mint, Ginger, cumin, mace, sumac, dill, nutmeg, and many more.

NATURAL AND ORGANIC TRENDS IN SPICE AND HERBS

Another trend in the modern spices includes the demand for natural spices and herbs. Since the demand for natural, organic and chemical free food has been on the rise for a better, healthier lifestyle, and for preventing disease and better environment.

Many sustainable methods have been adopted for growing crops without the use of harmful chemicals. Because of this trend, the demand of natural and organic spices is increasing among the consumers. Now, the organic spices are free from being genetically modified and synthetic fillers.

FORMS AND USES OF SPICE AND HERBS

Usually, spices are available in the following forms.

- Fresh spices
- Whole dried spices
- Dried and pre ground spices

Usually, spices are available in dried form and whole dried spices have a long shelf life, making it easier to store them for longer time periods. Herbs are available in dried or fresh form.

Herbs and spices have great importance in our way of living as an ingredient used in foods and beverages, perfumery, medicines, cosmetics and beauty, and as a plant in the garden. They are used in foods to infuse flavor, color and pungency. They have numerous uses for their antioxidant, nutritional and antimicrobial properties. They have been made to develop pure essential oils, which is a growing industry in today's world.

As for the application of spices and herbs is concerned, they provide a vast spectrum of flavorings, aromas and tastes such as sweet, spicy, savory, bitter, pungent or sour notes to the foods and beverages.

Various uniquely balanced curry blends are used in Indian cuisines. Chinese cuisine includes a contrast among sour,

12

sweet and pungent notes. So, whether you are creating fusion or authentic themes, or you are adding heat to your regular traditional food; spices are the fundamental principles of texture, taste, flavor and visual appeal.

The next chapter includes various numbers of herbs and spice blends used in various cuisines including, Asian, Europeans, Mediterranean, African, North American, Italian, and Mexican, etc.

BLENDS OF SPICES AND HERBS FROM AROUND THE WORLD

The following chapter consists of a compilation of spice blends and mixes from cuisines around the world so that you can enjoy the most exotic flavors in the comfort of your own home made with the easiest mixes, rather than buying the pre-made mixes from the store.

ASIAN HERBS AND SPICE MIXES/BLENDS

Chinese Five Spice Mix

Chinese Five Spice Mix includes all the five flavors in it, i.e. sweet, bitter, salty, sour and pungent. This mix brings spicy-sweet and warm flavors to roasted meats and stir-fries.

Ingredients

    4 star anise, whole

4 teaspoons generic peppercorns

2 teaspoons cloves

2 teaspoons fennel

2 teaspoon coriander seeds

2 cinnamon sticks, broken

Directions

1. Heat a dry pan over medium heat, toast all the ingredients except for cinnamon until aromatic and fragrant. Slowly toss the ingredients and allow them to cool for some time.

2. Grind the toasted ingredients and cinnamon in a spice grinder for 20 seconds to turn them into a fine powdered form.

3. Store in a sealed jar.

Shichimi Togarashi

Shichimi Togarashi is a Japanese spice mixture comprising of seven ingredients. It is often used in noodles, soup (for example to a miso soup) and rice products. Also you can use this mix as a topping for grilled meat or fish, like tuna and salmon, at the beginning or the end of cooking.

Suggestion: Blend Shichimi Togarashi Mix with olive oil (in proportions as you prefer) to make a marinade for chicken breast.

Ingredients

    1 tablespoon black peppercorns

    1 tablespoon tangerine peel, dry

    1 tablespoon red chili peppers, ground

    2 tablespoons nori, flakes

    2 teaspoons sesame seeds

    2 teaspoons black cannabis seeds

    2 teaspoons garlic, minced

Directions

1. Grind all the ingredients until chunky.

2. Store in a sealed jar and refrigerate for a month.

Use when required.

Gomashio (Toasted Sesame Salt)

Gomashio is a dry condiment made from unhulled sesame seeds and salt. Used as a replacement for salt
It is used as a topping for sekihan or sprinkled over plain rice, stews, soups and vegetables.

Ingredients

    1 cup sesame seeds

    ½ tablespoon sea salt

Directions

1. Toast the sesame seeds in a skillet over a medium heat for 10-12 minutes, stirring constantly till they become light brown and aromatic.
2. Put the toasted seeds and salt in a spice grinder and grind into a coarse meal.
3. Let it cool and then, transfer to an airtight glass jar.

Basic Curry Spice Mix

Basic Curry Spice Mix is the basis for many of the curries that are restaurant style. These curries are rich in antioxidant species and are the ideal food.

Curry is perfect for most dishes. This spice is used for sauces and for meat dishes, especially for poultry, pork and mutton. But most frequently it is used to flavor rice, which takes its yellow color.

Ingredients

    1/2 cup Paprika

    1/4 cup Cumin

    1 tablespoon Fennel Powder

    2 Tablespoons Fenugreek powder

    2 tablespoons Ground Mustard Powder

    1 tablespoon ground Red Pepper Flakes

    3 tablespoons ground Coriander

    1/4 cup ground Turmeric root

    1 tablespoon ground Cardamom

    1 teaspoon Cinnamon Powder

    1/2 teaspoon Cloves Powder

Directions

1. Mix all ingredients well in a bowl or blend in a food blender.

2. Add the blended mixture in an airtight container or a jar, and use it to the needs.

Garam Masala

Garam means hot. Garam Masala is common in South Asian and North Indian cuisines, which can be used either alone or with other seasonings. This mixture is not as spicy as chili mix, however, is usually aromatic and bitter.

Garam Masala is typically used for seasoning meats, but also can be successfully used as a supplement to sauces and marinades. Sometimes it is added to fried dough and batters. Add Garam Masala at the end of cooking. Its clear and sharp flavor penetrates the entire dish.

Toasted Garam Masala should be used immediately. Leftovers should be closed tightly and stored for no longer than six months.

Ingredients
   3 tablespoons cardamom powder
   2 tablespoons cinnamon powder
   ¼ cup ground cloves
   ¼ cup black pepper
   2 teaspoons cumin powder
   1 teaspoon coriander powder
   ½ teaspoon nutmeg, freshly grated

Directions

1. Toast the ingredients in a pan over a medium heat till aromatic.
2. Allow to cool and store in an airtight jar.

Vinegar Spice Blend

Vinegar spice blend is a convenient and easy way to add flavor to marinades, sauces, rubs and salads. It can be used as a sprinkle for vegetables and meat.

Ingredients

    1 cup rice vinegar

    1 teaspoon coriander seed

    1 teaspoon cloves

    3 whole star anise

    1 teaspoon fresh ginger, minced

    1 lemon

    1 teaspoon peppercorns

    5 cilantro stems, fresh

Directions

1. Add the first 5 ingredients in a saucepan, simmer them over low heat for 5-7 minutes, and let the mixture cool for a while.
2. Pour the mixture in a wide mouth jar, cover the jar and keep it aside for 2 weeks stirring occasionally.
3. Strain the mixture through a muslin cloth into a glass jar.
4. Add lemon slices, peppercorns and cilantro.

MIDDLE EASTERN SPICE BLENDS

Baharat

Baharat is an all-purpose seasoning, commonly used in Middle Eastern Cuisines. Baharat adds flavor and depth to tomato sauces, soups, rice pilafs, couscous and lentils. It can be added to meat (especially to lamb), fish and poultry.

This mixture is great for barbecues. Rub meat and vegetables before grilling. Fits perfectly to the eggplant.

Baharat is the equivalent of the Indian Garam Masala and has the same application. Use it at the end of cooking to enhance the aroma and taste.

To disperse the aroma, blend a teaspoon of the Bahrat mixture with a little bit of butter before frying.

Ingredients

¼ teaspoon ground cloves

¼ teaspoon ground cardamom

2 teaspoons paprika

2 teaspoons ground cumin

1 teaspoon ground black pepper

1 teaspoon ground coriander

½ teaspoon ground cinnamon

½ teaspoon ground nutmeg

Directions

Combine the ingredients in a bowl and store the mixture in a glass jar.

Egyptian Dukkah Spice Mix

Egyptian Dukkah Spice Mix is an Egyptian condiment, comprising of nuts, herbs and spices. The spice mix is used as a dip with fresh vegetables and bread. It can be sprinkled on pasta, roasted vegetables, peaches and feta cheese.

Ingredients

2 tablespoons roughly ground almonds

2 tablespoons pistachios, roughly chopped

2 tablespoons sesame seeds

4 teaspoon cumin seeds, roughly grounded

4 teaspoon coriander seeds, ground

½ teaspoon salt

Directions

Toast all the spices on a medium heat in a pan, let them cool and then, store in an airtight jar away from light.

Moroccan Spice Mix

Moroccan Spice Mix can be the best addition to chicken, tuna, swordfish, stews, meat and vegetables. It adds aroma and extra flavor to your meals without adding additional fat.

Ingredients

  1 teaspoon Hungarian sweet paprika

  1/2 teaspoon ground cumin

  1/2 teaspoon ground cinnamon

  1/4 teaspoon salt

  1/4 teaspoon ground ginger

  1/4 teaspoon ground red pepper

  1/4 teaspoon black pepper, freshly crushed

Directions

1. Add all the ingredients in a blender. Pulse to combine well.

2. Use this rub for meat and vegetable dishes.

3. This spice mix is ideal for grilling.

EUROPEAN SPICE BLENDS

French Fines Herbs

French Fines Herbes forms a mainstay of French cuisines. It is commonly used in egg-dishes, but it is a good addition to lighter-flavored fish.

Use fresh herbs

Ingredients

    2 tablespoon parsley, chopped

    2 tablespoon chervil, chopped

    1 tablespoons thyme, finely chopped

    2 tablespoon chives, snipped

    4 teaspoon tarragon, chopped

Directions

Chop the herbs right before using the mixture, always make it fresh for amazing flavors.

Basic Herbe De Provence

Herbes de Provence is a seasoning mixture of many herbs that grow abundantly in southern France. This mixture makes a great seasoning for vegetables, fish and grilled meats.

Ingredients

4 tablespoons thyme, dried

2 tablespoon savory, dried

1 tablespoon marjoram, dried

4 tablespoons rosemary, dried

1 tablespoon lavender flowers, dried

Directions

Combine all the herbs and keep in an airtight jar in dark place.

Khmeli-Suneli Spice Mix

Khmeli Suneli is a traditional Georgian spice mix. Khmeli Suneli provides an amazing flavor and aroma to roasted vegetables, beans, meat dishes and stews.

Ingredients

1 tablespoon marjoram, dried

1 tablespoon dill, dried

1 tablespoon mint, dried

1 tablespoon summer savory dried

1 tablespoon parsley, dried

1 tablespoon coriander, ground

½ teaspoon dried fenugreek leaves + ½ teaspoon fenugreek seeds

1 teaspoon marigold petals, dried

½ teaspoon black pepper powder

2 bay leaves, crushed

Directions

Combine all the spices and herbs together and use them in your soups and stews.

Italian Spice Mix

Italian Spice Mix is a good way to add extra flavor to pasta sauce. If stored in an air-tight container, it can be used for 12 weeks.

Ingredients

    1/2 cup Basil leaf

    1/2 cup Marjoram Leaf

    1/2 cup Oregano leaf

    1/4 cup cut and sifted Rosemary Leaf

    1/4 cup Thyme Leaf

    2 tablespoons Garlic Powder

Directions

1. Place all herbs in a jar.
2. Shake well and it's ready to use.

French Onion Soup Spice Mix

French Onion Soup Spice Mix provides you soups and dinners in the easiest and fastest way.

Ingredients

¾ cup dried onion flakes

2 teaspoons onion powder

2 teaspoons garlic powder

1 teaspoon sea salt

1 ½ teaspoon dried parsley

1 teaspoon turmeric

Directions

1. Combine the spices together and use while making the soup.
2. Combine these ingredients in 1/2 cup of sour cream and ½ cup of mayonnaise.

Fajita Seasoning Mix

Fajita seasoning mix is an authentic Mexican blend that makes delicious fajitas in no time. It has a mouthwatering, well-balanced flavor.

Ingredients

1/4 cup chili powder

2 tablespoons Sea Salt

2 tablespoons Paprika

1 tablespoon onion powder

1 tablespoon Garlic Powder

1 teaspoon cayenne powder

1 tablespoon cumin powder

Directions

Mix well in a bowl and store in airtight container until use.

Taco Seasoning

Taco Seasoning has a Mexican origin. Homemade taco seasoning is both nutritious, as well as cheap. It adds taste to meats, fish, poultry, vegetables.

Ingredients

1/4 cup Chili Powder

1/4 cup Cumin Powder

1 Tablespoon Garlic powder

1 Tablespoon Onion powder

1 teaspoon Oregano powder

1 tablespoon Paprika

1/4 cup Sea salt

1 teaspoon ground pepper

Directions

1. Combine all the ingredients in a blender and mix well. Pulse until properly mixed.
2. Store it in an airtight jar for about six months.
3. The recipe serves you with approximately one cup.

Greek Spice Mix

Greek Spice Mix is a blend of different spices and herbs. It is used for the seasoning of ground meats and homemade pita chips.

Ingredients

   2 tablespoons dried oregano

   5 teaspoons onion powder

   5 teaspoons garlic powder

   1 tablespoon salt

   1 tablespoon black pepper, freshly ground

   1 tablespoon bouillon granules, beef-flavored

   1 tablespoon dried parsley

   1 teaspoon ground cinnamon

   1 teaspoon nutmeg, freshly ground

Directions

1. Combine all ingredients well and store in an airtight jar or a container.
2. Keep in a cool and dark place.

LATIN AMERICAN/CARIBBEAN SPICE MIX

Adobo Spice Mix

Adobo spice mix is Mexican in origin and is used as a rub for chicken, pork and fish.

Ingredients

- 2 Tablespoon salt
- 1 Tablespoon Paprika powder
- 1 Teaspoon garlic powder
- 1 Teaspoon chili powder
- 2 Teaspoon freshly ground black peppers
- 1 ½ Teaspoon onion powder
- 1 ½ Teaspoon dried oregano
- 1 ½ Teaspoon dried oregano

Directions

Stir all the spices together in a bowl and store in a sealed jar in a cool dark place.

Berbere Spice Mix (African)

Berbere is a chili spice mix, which is used to season almost everything from vegetables to meat and stews.

Ingredients

½ teaspoon fenugreek, freshly ground

½ cup ground Mexico chilies

¼ cup paprika

1 teaspoon ginger powder

1 teaspoon onion powder

½ teaspoon coriander powder

¼ teaspoon nutmeg powder

¼ teaspoon garlic powder

1/8 teaspoon ground cloves

1/8 teaspoon cinnamon powder

1/8 teaspoon allspice powder

Directions

1. Combine the mixture together and keep in an airtight jars.
2. Use this mixture in your meals including, vegetables, stews and stir fry.

DRY SPICE MIX RECIPES FOR RUBS, DRESSINGS, BEVERAGES AND SAUCES

Recipes of some of the popular spice mixes from around the world are already mentioned in the above chapter. You can easily give an exotic taste to your dishes by following the steps.

The following recipes include spice mixes that can be used for dressing, sauces, dips, rubs, marinades in advance to save time.

Just take the mix out and sprinkle it, or make it into a paste by combining with different liquid and cream ingredients.

SPICE RUBS FOR MEAT, POULTRY AND FISH

Jamaican Jerk Spice Rub

Jamaican Jerk Spice Rub is a very hot spice mixture, which is applied to chicken, fish, seafood, meat and pork,

Ingredients

1 tablespoon onion flakes

2 teaspoons ground thyme

1 teaspoon dried parsley

¼ teaspoon ground cinnamon

1 teaspoon ground black pepper

½ teaspoon cayenne pepper

1 teaspoon all spice powder

1 teaspoon paprika

½ teaspoon hot pepper flakes

¼ teaspoon ground cumin

1 tablespoon garlic powder

2 teaspoons salt

¼ teaspoon ground nutmeg

2 teaspoons sugar

2 teaspoons dried chives

Directions

1. Mix together and use when required.

2. Use 1 ½ tablespoon of seasoning for each pound of meat.

Poultry Seasoning Rub

Poultry Seasoning Rub is used not only to season chicken, turkey and stuffing, but also pot pies, meat or veggie burgers, soups and more.

Ingredients

    1 teaspoon salt

    1 teaspoon white pepper

    1 teaspoon smoked paprika

    1 teaspoon dry mustard

    ½ teaspoon bay leaves, dried

    1 teaspoon garlic powder

Directions

1. Put all the ingredients in a jar and shake well.
2. Rub well into the poultry before baking, roasting, grilling or putting in a slow cooker.

Fish Spice Mix

Fish Spice Mix Is used to add flavor to fish that will be fried, baked or grilled.

Ingredients

    1 tablespoon dried basil

    1 tablespoon dried crushed rosemary

    1 tablespoon dried parsley

    2 teaspoons sea salt

    2 teaspoons freshly ground peppers

    2 teaspoons ground dried ginger

    2 teaspoons dried thyme

    2 teaspoon dried marjoram

    1 teaspoon dried oregano

    1 teaspoon celery salt

    1 teaspoon garlic powder

Directions

1. Combine all the herbs and spices in a mixing bowl until properly blended.
2. Store in an airtight container.
3. Rub on the fish before grilling or baking.

Tuscan Spice Rub

Tuscan Spice Rub is used to season pork and roasted vegetables and add flavors to tomato sauces.

Ingredients

  2 tablespoon fennel seeds

  8 tablespoons dried basil

  4 tablespoons garlic powder

  4 tablespoons coarse salt

  3 tablespoons dried rosemary

  3 tablespoons dried oregano

Directions

1. Coarsely grind fennel seeds by pulsing them in a spice grinder or mortar and pestle.
2. Add the freshly ground fennel with the rest of ingredients in a jar. Shake them well to combine them properly and keep the container in a dry and dark place.
3. Use this rub on boneless chicken, salmon or any other meat. You can also use it with vegetable dishes.

SALAD DRESSINGS

Italian Dressing Spice Mix

Italian Dressing Spice Mix is a delicious blend of garlic and herbs, which can be used as a dressing, dip, rub, seasoning or marinade.

Suggestion: Blend the mixture with a Greek yoghurt to get an amazing dip to salads, raw vegetables, French fries.

Ingredients

    1 1/2 teaspoon garlic powder

    1 Tablespoon onion powder

    2 teaspoon oregano

    1 Tablespoon dried parsley

    2 teaspoons sea salt

    1 teaspoon pepper

    1/4 teaspoon thyme

Directions

1. Shake ingredients well and store in a jar.
2. Cook with some oil and enjoy on your salads.

Thousand Island Dressing Mix

Thousand Island dressing mix is added in cheeses and meats for chef's salad. It is great with substantial greens.

Ingredients

 1 cup mayonnaise

 1/3 cup ketchup

 1/4 cup pickle relish

 1 Tablespoon minced onion

 1 hard-boiled egg, chopped

Directions

Mix the ingredients well, put them in a glass container, and refrigerate them.

Creamy Garlic Dressing Mix

Creamy garlic dressing mix can be added to salads, French fries, meats and vegetables.

Ingredients

1 cup of milk

1 cup fresh parsley chopped

3 cloves of garlic minced

1 cup of mayonnaise

1 tablespoon dried dill

Salt and pepper, to taste

Directions

1. Blend parsley, garlic cloves in a blender.
2. Pour mixture into a bowl and add the remaining set of ingredients.
3. Whisk until blended well.

Oriental Dressing Mix

Oriental dressing mix is used as a seasoning, marinade or dip.

Ingredients

    1/4 cup vegetable oil

    1 tablespoon sesame oil

    1 tablespoon Rice vinegar

    1 tablespoon Soy sauce

    1/2 teaspoon Ground ginger

    1/2 teaspoon Sugar

Directions

Mix all oils together, add the ingredients, and mix well.

Ranch Dressing Mix

Ranch dressing mix is used to season chicken or fries, and is used to make skinny Greek yogurt ranch dip and ranch dressing.

Ingredients

    2 tablespoon Onion powder

    1/8 teaspoon Garlic powder

    1 tablespoon dried parsley

Directions

1. In a medium skillet, toast the mix on medium heat.

2. Let it cool and transfer to a jar.

3. To make the dressing, take your mixture out and add 1 cup of mayonnaise and buttermilk each.

DESSERTS AND BEVERAGE

Pumpkin Pie Spice Mix

Pumpkin pie spice mix is used to make delicious pumpkin pie desserts, cakes, beverages, smoothies, vanilla cream and sweet potato products.

Ingredients

    1/4 cup freshly ground cinnamon

    2 tablespoons freshly ground ginger

    2 teaspoons freshly ground nutmeg

    1 teaspoon ground cloves

Directions

1. In a small bowl, mix all the spices together.

2. Pour into an airtight container.

3. Use any time a recipe calls for pumpkin pie spice mix.

Spiced Mix for Hot Beverages

Spiced mix for hot beverages is used in several drinks in fall or winter: to milk, hot chocolate, coffee.

Ingredients

    4 ½ cup dark brown sugar

    1 ½ cinnamon, ground

    1 tablespoon ground ginger

    1 teaspoon freshly ground nutmeg

    1 teaspoon ground mace

    1 teaspoon ground cloves

Directions

1. Dry the brown sugar on a baking parchment for 2 to 3 hours to prevent clumping.

2. Add all the ingredients in the spice grinder. Pulse until the mixture is combined well.

3. Store in an airtight container to make hot spice beverages.

4. Heat 1 cup of cider (any cider of your choice) with 1 tablespoon of the mix.

5. Steep for 5-7 minutes.

6. For spices, coffee or hot cocoa, add 1 tablespoon of the mix for each cup.

7. Garnish your drink with whipped cream.

Dry Spice Mix for Tea

A mixture of dry spices is used to make tea that tastes like heaven, especially if you are stressed.

Ingredients

    1 tablespoon nutmeg powder

    1 tablespoon ginger powder

    ½ tablespoon cardamom powder

    1 tablespoon black pepper powder

    1 tablespoon cinnamon powder

    1 tablespoon cloves powder

Directions

1. Mix spice together in a bowl and transfer the mixture to an airtight jar to make tea.
2. Make black tea from a tea bag with hot water.
3. Add a pinch of spice mix into the tea.
4. Add milk of your choice.

Dry Spice Mix for Breads and Cakes

A mixture of dry spices is used to brew delicious breads and cakes. This dry spice mix enhances the flavors of these items.

Ingredients

3/4 teaspoon ground cardamom

3/4 teaspoon cinnamon

1/4 teaspoon ground ginger

1/4 teaspoon allspice powder

3/4 teaspoon salt

Directions

1. Combine the mixture and place in an airtight container.
2. Use the mixture when making spiced banana bread or chocolate cakes for a subtle spicy flavor.

SAUCES AND DIPS

Use the following in your pastas, snacks, rice recipes, and many more.

Korean Gochujang Sauce

Korean Gochujang Sauce is a savory condiment, which contain a lot of vitamins and minerals.
It can be used in marinades for meats, to punch up soups or stews.

Ingredients

> 5 tablespoons gochujang
>
> ½ teaspoon onion powder
>
> ½ teaspoon garlic powder
>
> 1 tablespoon sugar
>
> ¼ apple, shredded
>
> ¼ pear shredded
>
> 1 1/2 tablespoon lime juice, fresh
>
> 1 tablespoon sesame seeds, toasted
>
> 1 tablespoon corn syrup
>
> 1 tablespoon chili flakes

Directions

Combine all the ingredients in a mixing bowl, mix well and store in an airtight container.

Dry Cajun Spicy Dip Mix

Dry Cajun spicy dip mix is best when used as a dip for onion rings or sprinkled over potato and mixed in sauces.

Ingredients

    1 Tablespoon paprika

    3/4 teaspoon dried thyme

    3/4 teaspoon dried oregano

    3/4 teaspoon onion powder

    1/2 teaspoon cayenne pepper

    1/2 teaspoon garlic powder

    1/4 teaspoon pepper

    1/4 teaspoon Sugar

Directions

1. Combine ingredients in a bowl and stir to combine well. Place in a sealed jar.
2. To serve – combine the dip mix with 2 cups of sour cream. Stir till well blended. Cover and refrigerate for 8 hours or overnight.

Pickle Spice Mix

Pickling spice mix is added to pickles to enhance their flavor.

Ingredients
   1 cinnamon stick, broken into pieces

   2 dried bay leaves, crushed

   2 whole cloves

   2 tablespoons mustard seeds

   2 tablespoons whole coriander seeds

   1 tablespoon mixed peppercorns

   2 teaspoons whole allspice

   2 teaspoons dill seeds

   1 teaspoon red pepper flakes

Directions
1. In a small bowl, combine all the ingredients together.
2. Store in an airtight container at room temperature for up to 1 year. Use when needed.

Rice Seasoning/Spice Mix

Rice seasoning or spice mix is best when used to season rice.

Ingredients

½ cup parsley, dried

1 tablespoon dill

1 tablespoon basil

2 tablespoons onion powder

1 teaspoon pepper

1 cup almonds, coarsely chopped

Directions

1. Mix together all the ingredients.
2. Store in an airtight container.
3. To make 1 cup of rice, combine 2 cups of water and 3 tablespoons of seasoning mix and cook.

Dry Barbecue Sauce Spice Mix

Dry barbeque sauce spice mix is used as a marinade or a dip for barbeque items.

Ingredients
½ cup brown sugar

¼ cup paprika

¼ cup sea salt

1 tablespoon garlic powder

2 teaspoons onion powder

2 tablespoon chili powder

2 tablespoons black pepper powder

1 tablespoon dried sage

1 teaspoon allspice powder

1 teaspoon cumin powder

¼ teaspoon cayenne

1/8 teaspoon clove powder

Directions
1. Spread brown sugar on a baking paper and air dry it for 2 hours.
2. Sift all the ingredients in a bowl and mix them well.

3. Use this mixture to dry rub any meat that you want to grill or roast.

To make the Sauce

This same spice mix can be used to make barbeque sauce for your grilled meat or pulled chicken.

1. In a large saucepan, add ½ cup white vinegar, 1 tablespoon yellow mustard, 2 tablespoons of honey, 2 cups tomato ketchup, and 2 tablespoons of barbecue spice mix. Bring the mixture to boil over a medium heat. Let it simmer for 60-70 minutes at low-medium heat and stir the mixture occasionally.
2. Let it cool and store in the refrigerator.

Coconut-Spice Mix

Coconut spice mix is added to different sauces or as a dip for chicken, meat and vegetables.

Suggestion: Blend 1-2 teaspoon of Coconut spice mix with 1 cup of natural yoghurt or Greek yoghurt and 3 teaspoon of mayonnaise. The light version: no mayonnaise.

Ingredients

½ cup coconut powder

2 tablespoon lemon powder

2 teaspoons red chili flakes

I teaspoon ground coriander

½ teaspoon garlic powder

½ teaspoon salt

Directions

1. Mix the ingredients together and keep in a sealed glass container.
2. To make the sauce, add the spice mix in your pasta and noodles, and make it into a dip by adding in mayonnaise or sour cream.

Dry Spice Mix For Tomato Sauce

This dry spice mix is used to add extra aroma and flavor to tomato sauce.

Ingredients

    1 cup onion powder

    1 tablespoon garlic powder

    1 teaspoon thyme powder

    1 1/2 cups tomato powder from sun-dried tomatoes

    1 teaspoon salt

    1 teaspoon black pepper powder

    1 tablespoon basil powder

Directions

1. Combine the dry spices together and keep in a sealed container.
2. To make a sauce cook the spices in ¼ cup of olive oil and eat with pasta, noodles or noodle salads.

MAKE YOUR OWN UNIQUE SPICE AND HERB BLENDS

Spices and herbs have a colorful array of flavors and aroma in them. They can be mixed and matched to come up with your own personal blends. If you love spices and have a bunch of spices and herbs in your kitchen cabinet, you have an unlimited supply of amazing flavors. All you need is understanding about the flavor profile of various herbs and spices. Then you can add spicy, smoky, warm, sweet, aromatic and calming punch into your food and beverages.

In the beginning, you should experiment with the blend recipes mentioned in the earlier chapters of this book. Gradually, try to understand different forms of spices and you will see that the intensity of the flavors of the spices change as the spices change in form. You will learn that a freshly ground spice can have more flavor and aroma than a powdered one. If you are a beginner, you can start with powdered spices, then you can move on to the whole spices as you understand the strength and aroma changes of spices.

UNDERSTANDING THE CHARACTERISTIC OF SPICES AND HERBS

As the basic function of spices is their aroma, color and flavor, their specific chemical compounds are the reason for their unique properties. You can learn about the basic flavor the spices and herbs have, such as hot, earthy, warm, nutty, spicy, bitter, floral, herbaceous, piney, etc. An individual can identify the four most well-known flavor profiles. These are bitter, sour, salty and sweet. As you experiment with the spices, you will be able to make flavorful changes in any spice mix recipes to fit to your palate.

Spices have the following sensory characteristics. A single spice can have more than one sensory characteristic.

- Bitter
- Cooling
- Earthy
- Floral
- Fruity
- Hot
- Nutty
- Piney
- Pungent
- Sour

- Spicy
- Sweet
- Sulfuric
- Woody

FLAVOR PAIRING OF DIFFERENT SPICES

A person's creation of food is inspired by the flavor. When one understands the individual flavors of the ingredients, his dish will turn out better every time. Use a light hand for the first time, even when following a recipe as every person's receptors are unique and should be tailored to his palate. Never be hesitant to take a recipe and transform it with new and exciting flavors. In order to help you jump into the world of spice and start experimenting with your spice mixes, you should follow the following chart to understand different pairings of spices.

- Basil pairs well with capers, cilantro, chives, garlic, thyme, oregano, mint, marjoram, onion, parsley, and rosemary. Sweet basil goes well with pesto and tomato salads.

- Bay leaf goes well with artichokes, oregano, beans, savory, juniper, thyme, nuts, and sage.

- Allspice combines well with cardamom, cinnamon, cloves, coriander, ginger, juniper, mustard, nuts, and nutmeg.

- Cardamom pairs well with turmeric, saffron, star anise, clove, coriander, cumin, fennel seeds, chili, cinnamon, paprika, peppers, and mustard.

- Chives blend well with dill, cilantro, basil, parsley, tarragon and paprika.

- Cinnamon combines beautifully with mint, ginger, turmeric, turmeric, nutmeg, vanilla, chilies, and star anise.

- Cloves can be paired with cacao, cumin, ginger, star anise, nutmeg, fennel, and mace.

- Coriander pairs well with cloves, cumin, fennel, garlic, onion, parsley, mint, and nutmeg.

- Cumin could be combined with allspice, star anise, bay leaves, cardamom, cilantro, parsley, ginger, fennel, garlic, and fenugreek.

- Dill pairs well with basil, star anise, chives, coriander, fennel, garlic, cumin, ginger, mint, oregano, and parsley.

- Fennel combines beautifully with anise, basil, cilantro, cinnamon, dill, cumin, thyme, garlic, and fenugreek.

- Garlic can be combined with basil, chili, coriander, cumin, curry leaves, marjoram, mustard seeds, oregano, parsley, rosemary, and thyme.

- Ginger combines pretty well with cilantro, cinnamon, fennel, onion, nutmeg, cloves, coriander, vanilla, and turmeric.

- Mace goes well with spices such as vanilla, cinnamon, cloves, ginger, allspice, nutmeg, vanilla, and cumin.

- Rosemary combines well with onion, thyme, parsley, oregano, basil, fennel, garlic, and marjoram.

- Sage pairs well with bay leaf, ginger, onion, marjoram, parsley, paprika, thyme, and rosemary.

- Sesame flavors go well with garlic, ginger, and thyme.

SPICE MIX TOOLS AND SUPPLIES

It doesn't take a lot of tools and supplies to make your spice mixes and blends. As a basic, you need to purchase bottles of spice and herbs available in individual containers, measuring spoons and cups. Additional, you will need jars or cans to store your spice mixes.

In order to make spice blends, invest in a good electric grinder. You can also experiment with mortar and pestle. You will see that there is a slight flavor difference between spices when they are ground in a mortar and pestle as compared to an electric grinder.

For better flavors, use mortar and pestle if you want to roughly grind your spices. For making fine powders, use an electric grinder.

TIPS FOR MAKING AND STORING YOUR OWN SPICE MIX

By following these tricks, tips and guidelines, you will be able to keep the flavor of your spice mixes better and store them for a longer time period.

- Buy spices in whole form. Grind them right before making the mix fresh and more potent with intense flavors.

- Learn spice toasting as toasting spice before grinding them releases more flavor.

- Spice mixes such as curry blend and those containing cayenne, paprika, chili powder and red pepper, should be refrigerated to extend their potency.

- Before adding to the mix, crush the dried herb with the palm of your hands to release oil and produce a better flavor.

- Purchase herbs and spices sold in tin cans and avoid those which are sold in plastic as the plastic bags are not completely airtight and allow the light to enter.

- Make batches that you can use up within 3 months. Store the batches in the airtight glass containers and in a cool and dry space as light moisture and heat are the worst spice enemies.

CONCLUSION

I hope this book was able to help you to know about spices from around the world and their magical flavors that can make your food delicious and irresistible.

No doubt the world of spices and herbs is a vast, colorful and aromatic world of flavors and healing. Spices have been used in ancient civilizations and since the beginning of the mankind. They had been used to preserve meats, and also to heal injuries and diseases. In earlier times, the spices were considered a valuable item of trade since some parts of the world did not have an abundance supply of these spices and herbs.

But now in modern times, everyone can enjoy the flavor of spices and herbs from around the world as these are available everywhere. You can add an oriental, Moroccan, Italian, Asian or any punch of flavors to your meals.

The flavor you can get from blending your own spices is far better than the one provided in MSG filled processed spice mixes. So, have fun with spices and blend away. You don't have to be an expert to start your own spice mixes. Start by understanding a few spices and learn along the way.

FROM THE AUTHOR
I would like to ask you for a small favor.
Book reviews are very important for other spice mixes enthusiasts like you. If you have a minute, please leave a comment under my book.
Thank You!

Check Out My Other Book

Bellow you will find my other book that are popular on Kindle.

Sauces, Salsa And Dips Recipes: The Most Delicious Original Recipes From Around The World

Best regards!

Printed in Great Britain
by Amazon